How it points to Jesus,
To our Destinies,
and to the Destiny
of our Nation!

$\mathcal{D}$estiny
OF A
TREE

BY LARRY V. CURNEAL

~~three~~ Josiah —
Thank you so much for all your
support and encouragement given to me in
the writing of Destiny. I hope that you
enjoy the journey, and that the Lord
speaks to you along the way!
In Christ's Love,
Larry

TRILOGY

PROFESSIONAL PUBLISHING MEETS POWERFUL PROMOTION

A wholly owned subsidiary of **TBN**

Destiny of a Tree

Trilogy Christian Publishers A Wholly Owned Subsidiary of Trinity Broadcasting Network

2442 Michelle Drive Tustin, CA 92780

Book illustrations by Earl Coon

For information about special discounts for bulk purchases, please contact Trilogy Christian Publishing.

Trilogy Disclaimer: The views and content expressed in this book are those of the author and may not necessarily reflect the views and doctrine of Trilogy Christian Publishing or the Trinity Broadcasting Network.

Manufactured in the United States of America

10 9 8 7 6 5 4 3 2 1

Library of Congress Cataloging-in-Publication Data is available.

Readers are encouraged to go to www.destinyofatree.com to contact the author or to find information as to how to buy this book in bulk at a discounted rate.

Subjects: Christion Fiction / Christian Living / Inspirational / Spirituality

ISBN: 978-1-68556-565-7

E-ISBN: 978-1-68556-566-4

How it points to *Jesus*,
to our *destinies*,
and to the *destiny*
of our *nation*!

DEDICATION

I dedicate this book to the revelations that God has given to me through the Holy Spirit.

I also wish to dedicate this book to my wife, Carol, who was an inspiration through the course of writing this book and ultimately helped in editing it.

ACKNOWLEDGMENTS

I would like to express my deepest thanks to the following people:

First, I would like to bestow my undying (literally) gratitude to my lovely wife, Carol, and our nurse daughter, Lee-Ann Bronikowski, for nursing me back to good health five years ago. My utmost gratitude also goes to my primary care physician, Douglas Spence, MD, my surgeon, Jay Starr, MD, my nephrologist, Jamshid Amanzadeh, and the other members of the medical team. Without all the patience, skill, and tender loving care of all the above, this book would have never been finished.

Thanks go to our computer tech son, Joseph, for all the encouragement, for putting all the fragmented pieces of the manuscript into a manageable file, and then outsourcing it for final typing, editing, and cover illustrations. Joe's expertise also became invaluable in obtaining the proper copyright and in the marketing of the finished product.

In as much as this has been a Curneal Family Production, I wish to thank our son, Brian, of Fort Worth, Texas, for his assistance and know-how about setting up a proper title page. Also, the wonderful short stories and movie scripts that Brian has written were a great inspiration for me to try my hand at doing some writing myself! I also wish to thank our daughter, Heather Brookhouse of Brookhouse Photography, Sherwood, Oregon, for being such a source of encouragement to me through all the wonderful phone conversations as well as messages on birthday and Father's Day cards through the years.

Many thanks go to David Davis, Jr., for permission to use an illustration of his ten-foot cross at the end of our book. This beautiful cross, which he constructed of rough-cut cedar and inscribed with all the descriptive names of Jesus found in the Bible, was beautifully illustrated by Kalkaska portrait artist Earl Coon, who did all of the lovely line drawings for *Destiny of a Tree*. Earl, it was another *divine appointment* that God put us together!

My heartfelt thanks also go out to Earl's lovely helpmate, Juanita Coon, whose loving encouragement and support of both Earl's drawings and of my writings helped bring forth the transition of the destiny story from a dream into a reality! I thank God for using her to bring Earl and me together so his illustrations could bring the destiny journey to life!

Many thanks also go to Ken Kreh and Pastor James

Martin, two of my fellow Keryx Prison Ministry team members, who are also published authors. Their wonderful books were a great inspiration, and their words of encouragement a tremendous blessing to me! I would also like to thank my lumberjack friend, Dean Pendock of Central Lake, Michigan, and his lovely Christa, for enlightening me about jack pine trees and other trees of the forest.

Speaking of *divine appointments*, I would also like to thank Bill Bustance of Trigger Boxing for his Guest Opinion article that appeared in the March 2nd, 2014, edition of the *Grand Traverse Insider*. The Lord used his wonderful article with its picture of a pair of boxing gloves to show me that He wanted the "An Appeal to Heaven Flag" story to be included as chapter 4 of this book!

My acknowledgment section would be incomplete if I failed to posthumously thank my parents for my wonderful Christian upbringing. I wish to especially thank my father, Clarence Jessie Curneal, for the inspiration I received by reading the wonderful short stories and novelette he wrote as a young man. I like to think that, in some way, I am fulfilling the hopes, dreams, and prayers that he had of becoming a published author.

Thanks most of all go to you, Carol, my wife, my

friend, and the love of my life, for editing and encouraging me to stick with it over the years despite the many fiery darts the enemy threw at us along the way. I could not have done it without the *Lord*, and I couldn't have done it without *you*!

TABLE OF CONTENTS

INTRODUCTION

And it shall come to pass in the last days, says
God, that I will pour out My Spirit on all flesh;
your sons and your daughters shall prophesy,
your young men shall see visions, your old men
shall dream dreams.

Acts 2:17 (NKJV)

In as much as I was seventy-one years old when I had
the dream that instigated this journey, I guess you could
say I don't regard myself as an "old man." I know I'm no
spring chicken, but I believe God has a lot of work for me
to do here, on planet earth, before I go on to glory!

I am not much of a dreamer, and whenever I do dream,
I usually can't recall it when I wake up. However, the
night of January 17th, 2013, was very different. I woke up
at 5 a.m. and found that I had been crying! I had witnessed
a "story" that touched me very deeply in my sleep.

The central character of the story was, of all things,
a tree, and the plot was about how this tree had fulfilled
its "destiny" while on earth. As improbable as this might
seem (i.e., an inanimate object having a destiny), the story depicted how the tree's "destiny" illustrated a spiritual

truth—sort of how Jesus used parables in the New Testament. The truth, thus explained as the story progressed, was that God indeed has a destiny planned for each of us, and we are not truly happy and fulfilled until we discover what that destiny is and begin walking in it. As I pondered this story, I was convinced that God wanted it told.

The question was "how?" and "in what format?" I am, by no stretch of the word, a "writer." Even though I enjoyed my English classes in high school and college, I have never had anything published. My occasional writings revolved around personal journaling and very short accounts of spiritual encounters over the years.

The more I thought about the story, the more I grasped that God was telling me that He wanted it conveyed through a piece of poetry. This kind of threw me because I had no prior training in poetry, and neither was I acquainted with it. Besides, my few meager attempts at the art were limited mostly to goofy poems to my lovely wife, Carol, scribbled on greeting cards and Christmas gift tags to make her laugh or, at least, roll her eyes at me!

Be that as it may, as time permitted, I began the arduous task of writing out the story in poetic form. It was slow at best; however, after much prayer, the Holy Spirit would give me one word with which to start a verse. And like clockwork, the rest of the verse would kind of fall in line. This recurred with every following verse, which, to my amazement, would ultimately rhyme with and complement the verse that preceded it! Three days later, I could boast of a completed poem with twelve four-line stanzas.

What happened in the subsequent days, weeks, and months was nothing short of amazing. The poem sort of took on a life of its own. Through a series of *divine appointments*, the Lord took me on a wonderful journey connecting His story with a radio interview, a world-famous poem, a world-famous song, a New York Times Best-Selling novel, an American Revolutionary flag, and a wonderful book about the world's greatest revivals. As these events unfolded, my wife sensed the Lord was telling her that they should be documented as a part of this story. Hence, the writing of *Destiny of a Tree* came into being, as seen in the pages of this book.

While the individual encounters and revelations were equally thrilling, one of them stood out: when God led me to study the central character of the story, the jack pine tree. Upon investigation, I startlingly found that this tree does, in fact, have a *destiny* in *real life*! Notably, the jack pine tree has unusual attributes that point to Jesus Christ in *nine different ways*!

I believe that this phenomenon is the true essence of this story: God has chosen to proclaim that His Son, Jesus, is the answer to all of this world's troubles in these last days through a simple pine tree! I hereby invite you, the reader, to join me as I attempt to fulfill *my* God-given destiny of relating this truly fantastic story!

As I type these pages, my prayer is that you see how God can and will guide, direct, and encourage you along the way in finding and fulfilling *your* destiny if you surrender your life to Him. Jeremiah 29:11 (TLB) states, "For I know the plans I have for you, says the Lord. They are plans for good and not for evil, to give you a future and a hope." God is not going to formulate plans for your future even before you were in the womb only to "leave you out to dry." He *wants* you to *live* in the *fullness* of the *life* He has designed *just* for *you*!

According to Dr. Charles F. Stanley, Senior Pastor of First Baptist Church in Northern Atlanta, Georgia, "Discovering God's purpose for your life is the surest path for success. None of us can foretell the great things He has in store for us, but we can trust His plan completely."[1]

"And it shall come to pass in the last days, says God, …

THE POEM

"Destiny of a Tree"

Awoken by the Lord at five in the morning.
Had to get up because soon I was crying.
Tears were flowing 'cause of what I saw;
Tears of joy, they continued to fall.

What I saw was beautiful to behold.
It was a story that *needs* to be told!
A story about the *destiny* of a tree,
And how it applies to *you* and to *me*.

You may ask, how can this ever be?
How could a *tree* have a *destiny*?
And how could such a tree's story
Tell about the destiny of *you* or *me*?

Each of us has a destiny to fit God's plan.
To fulfill it is the goal for woman and man.
To never fulfill God's plan for our life,
Is to live a life that could be full of strife.

In the Spirit, God took me to a cottage on a lake.
It was like a dream, but I was now totally awake.
Beside the cottage, I could see,
Halfway to the lake was one tree.

Some thirty feet tall with an open irregular crown,
Its scraggly appearance might cause one to frown.
With irregular shape, beauty it did lack.
'Twas not very pretty, this pine called *jack*.

The newly-wed couple was so very proud
Of their home, that they were riding on a cloud.
They loved each other with a love that wouldn't fade;
Loved the cottage, lake, and tree that gave them shade.

The jack pine tree stood to watch as their lives unfolded;
The comings and goings of busy lives were duly noted.
The seasons came, and the seasons went.
Days, weeks, and months were happily spent.

Picnics and barbecues were held near the faithful tree.
Then one day, the growing family numbered three.
Strange noises during the night could now be heard,
As Mom and Dad's sleep was now being disturbed!

Some time passed, and then some more.

One day, the family numbered four.

The hammock came down from branches where it had hung;

'Twas replaced by *tires* where the kids came and swung.

The tree faithfully stood as many more years passed by.

Birthdays and graduations came as the tree grew high.

Then one day came an *outdoor wedding*,

And before you knew it, *grandchildren* came swinging.

Throughout the many years, the noble jack pine tree

Contributed *much* to this growing happy family!

And through the years, this *tree* found *its* destiny,

Lord, please help *us* to *be* all that *we* can *be*!

CHAPTER ONE

Divine Appointment One

The Radio Interview

Waking up on the morning of January 18th, 2013, I lay in bed trying to process what had transpired during the night. Through my mind's eye, I reflected on the dream, which had dramatically affected me a few hours before. Then, a story began to emerge—a story involving a tree, which I believed to be a jack pine tree. Recalling the dream, God showed me how something as insignificant as a tree, not a very pretty one at that, could fulfill its "destiny" of bringing joy and happiness to a certain family.

My dream portrayed how the tree beside the cottage by the lake fulfilled its destiny: by being a vital element in the lives of a newly married couple, their children, and their grandchildren through the years. Moreover, via this portrayal, God illustrated how seemingly meaningless, unimportant lives can be transformed into rich, full lives through the guidance of the Holy Spirit, who guides us into the destiny that God planned for us before we were even conceived.

After further contemplation, I was convinced that He

wanted this story told. Besides, I also realized that this would mean treading a different path than He had ever taken me on before. You see, all the other stories that He had imparted me to write about were my own personal testimonies, accounts of supernatural healings, and occurrences in and of nature. This story, on the other hand, would be termed "fiction" because it is based on a dream rather than an actual occurrence, although it illustrates a spiritual truth—as did the other stories. In other words, this story would be like the many parables that Jesus told in the Bible to illustrate spiritual truths He was trying to get across.

While I was pondering all of this, I happened to turn on WLJN, a local Christian radio station, as is my daily routine while getting dressed; I happened to tune in just in time to catch the concluding part of a program whereby a young Christian author who had just finished his second book was being interviewed. When I realized that the topic of discussion was creativity in writing, I listened to the rest of the program, after which I played the rebroadcast of the entire interview.

I felt that this could be a "divine appointment" orchestrated by God when it was stated that the new book was a "diverse" story, i.e., a combination of truth and fiction—

the very kind of story that I felt the Lord was asking me to write!

It was pointed out in the interview that the "story," fact or fiction, has an unrivaled sway and appeal because it is capable of reaching people who might be impervious to other writing approaches. For instance, in the New Testament, Jesus told many "parables," defined by the Wester's Dictionary as "a usually short fictitious story that illustrates a moral attitude or a religious principle."

The interview additionally brought out that facts explain things; however, a *story* compels and captures not only the explanation but also the *emotion* and *mystery* of things. This reminded me of how Carol and I had been profoundly moved by movies such as *Field Of Dreams* and *The Natural*, both of which we found had spiritual undertones.

In summary, I believe that my turning on the radio just in time to hear this interview was truly a "divine appointment" ordained by God to encourage me to go ahead and write *this* kind of story.

"A tree that may in summer wear
a nest of robins in her hair;"

CHAPTER TWO

Divine Appointment Two

"Trees"

On February 2nd, 2013, Carol and I chose to watch the *Groundhog Day* movie since it was Groundhog Day. In the movie, Bill Murray decided to learn some French poetry in a bid to impress his co-worker. After the movie, Carol told me how much she loved poetry and that she could still recite parts of some of the poems she learned in her sixth-grade English class, such as "Trees" by Alfred Joyce Kilmer. She looked this poem up on the internet, and I was amazed at how it seemed to relate to *Destiny of a Tree*! Subsequently, Carol told me that she felt there was something very special about Kilmer's poem.

Later that evening, God led me to take another look at the Kilmer poem on my laptop. It did indeed seem very relevant to the poem God had given to me, so I did some digging on the author and how the poem came to be. I found that Joyce Kilmer was a prolific poet whose works celebrated the common beauty of the natural world and his

Roman Catholic faith. I also learned that Kilmer became immensely popular as a poet across the United States when "Trees" was published in a magazine. Robert Holliday, his friend and editor, stated that "Trees" speaks "with authentic song to the simplest of hearts." He also added that "the exquisite poem, now so universally known, made his [Kilmer's] reputation more than all the rest he had written put together."[2]

That evening, I was astounded by my findings on Joyce Kilmer and his signature poem, but there is one thing I couldn't have seen coming: Kilmer wrote "Trees" on February 2nd, 1913, *exactly a hundred years ago*—the *very day*—that the Lord brought the poem to our attention! There was no way I could have been prepared for that! At this juncture, I was convinced that there was indeed something extraordinary about this poem, considering that the Lord chose to make Carol remember it on its hundredth anniversary, and I couldn't wait to tell her that God had just given us another *divine appointment* on this journey!

When Carol and I recovered from the shock of this divine revelation from God, we concurred that the Lord wanted "Trees" included in the making of *Destiny of a Tree*, so here goes:

> I think I shall never see
> A poem as lovely as a Tree.
>
> A tree whose hungry mouth is pressed
> Against the earth's sweet flowing breast;
> A tree that looks at God all day,
> And lifts her leafy arms to pray;
>
> A tree that may in summer wear
> A nest of robins in her hair;
>
> Upon whose bosom snow has lain;
> Who intimately lives with rain.
>
> Poems are made by fools like me,
> But only God can make a tree.[3]

What's more, I noticed several similarities between Joyce Kilmer's "Trees" and "Destiny of a Tree" when I compared them. Both poems refer to God. "Trees" refers to the changing seasons of nature, while "Destiny of a

Tree" refers to the changing seasons of human life. Also, both were written in the rhyming-couplets rhyme scheme, i.e., the whole poem is comprised of couplets in which each pair of lines rhymes with each other. Finally, both poems use personification and imagery—the featured trees were given human attributes and characteristics.

Additionally, Kilmer's signature poem was turned into a song by Oscar Rasbach, an American pianist and composer, in 1922. Rasbach's works included two operettas and about twenty published songs, but his most significant musical composition was "Trees." It has also been performed and recorded by famous musicians, among which are Nelson Eddy, Robert Merrill, Mario Lanza, Sarah Vaughan, and The Platters. Moreover, Disney Studios did a beautifully animated movie rendition of the poem in 1948, sung by Fred Waring and The Pennsylvanians. The poem itself has also been included in several movies, such as *Superman II*, TV series such as *All In The Family*, and aired on various radio broadcasts. It's needless to say that "Trees" is a celebrated work of art. Therefore, by associating "Destiny of a Tree" with such a famous poem and in such a marvelous way, the Lord seemed to be saying that He has wonderful plans for the poem and the book, and I needed to be patient and wait upon Him to bring these plans to fruition.

CHAPTER THREE

Divine Appointment Three

"The Three Bells"

Four days later, on February 6th, the Lord gave me
another piece of the puzzle in making *Destiny of a Tree*.
I was channel-surfing that evening when I came across
a *Time Life* promo for Country Hits CDs. I watched this
program for about half an hour, enjoying the video clips of
some songs I had loved from the past.

Over the years, the Lord would have me experience a
"special feeling" whenever He wants to call my attention
to something. On this particular evening, I felt this distinct
feeling while watching one of the many clips aired on the
show. It was a song by The Browns, "The Three Bells." I
have always loved this song, even though it makes me cry
every time I hear it play.

Following up on the special feeling that the Lord had
given me, I looked into the song on the internet, and thus,
I discovered why it always makes me cry. Based on my
findings, I believe it is a song *truly anointed* by God. Additionally, I appreciated that, just like "Trees," it also has
a direct connection to "Destiny of a Tree."

The *Okzonia* website had the following to say about "The Three Bells:" "The song is nothing less than a beautiful philosophical meditation on the brevity and poignancy of our human lives—a kind of celebration of our mortality."[4] I believe that this song was inspired and anointed by God in that the little congregation in the song prayed for guidance from above, asked for the Lord's blessings, and prayed that it would not be led into temptation.

The Browns scored their *biggest hit ever* in 1959 when their folk-pop single, "The Three Bells," peaked at number one on the *Billboard Hot 100* pop and country charts. It also marked the first crossover hit of many of the accompanist Chet Adkins. The song spent ten weeks on the country charts and four weeks on the pop charts. The Browns' signature song has not only been recorded by at least a dozen individuals and musical groups in the country; it has also achieved international fame. "The Three Bells" was originally written in France in 1945 and has since been recorded in at least six different languages.

The connection of "The Three Bells" with "Destiny of a Tree" that I noted was three-fold. First, both spoke of God and His guidance through life. Secondly, both spoke of pine trees, while "Destiny of a Tree's" central character *is* a jack pine tree. Thirdly, the song documents *three* stages in the life of *one* person, and correspondingly, the poem speaks about *three* generations of *one* family!

As I thanked the Lord for giving me this divine appointment and touching my life again with this beautiful song, I began to wonder where He would take me next *on this wonderful journey*!

CHAPTER FOUR

Divine Appointment Four

The "An Appeal to Heaven" Flag

One day in March 2014, my wife and I received an email from our good friend, Melody Helfand, who lives on Drummond Island in Michigan's Upper Peninsula. The email had two videos attached which were of Dr. Douglas (Dutch) Sheets preaching at Pastor Chuck Pierce's church in Corinth, Texas.

I quickly realized that God had given me another "divine appointment" as I began watching the first video! He started his message by using an Everlast boxing glove as an illustration. I found this to be pretty amazing since I had a picture of a pair of boxing gloves *on my desk*—I had clipped it from an article published in the weekly Grand Traverse Insider *just the day before*! And little did I know that the article, with its picture of a pair of boxing gloves, would serve as the introduction to God's *divine appointment* of having me watch Dutch Sheet's videos!

Dutch began his sermon by describing a dream in which he is a boxer facing five giants in a boxing match that lasted five rounds. He consecutively knocked each of them out—one per round, each with one punch and alternating fists. As he knocked out the giants, representing strongholds that are attempting to rule and destroy America (abortion, violence, racism, various addictions, and sexual perversions), he noticed one of his boxing gloves had the word "everlast" printed on it, while the other glove had the word "evergreen."

For Dutch, the word "everlast" has two meanings, the first being the name of premier boxing equipment, and the second is *Olam El*—the Hebrew name for "the Everlasting God," who exists outside of time. However, the meaning of the "evergreen" on the other boxing glove eluded Dutch for six years until he was told about another dream in which he was presented with the "An Appeal to Heaven" flag—a white flag with an *evergreen tree* on it.

Before the Stars and Stripes existed, General George Washington commissioned several ships for the Revolutionary War effort, and each ship sailed under the "An Appeal to Heaven" banner, or Pine Tree Flag, as it came to be known. The phrase "An Appeal to Heaven," across the top of the flag, stems from the writings of John Locke, a mid-1600s English philosopher, who stated that human rights originate with God, not the government.

> Locke's phrase, 'Appeal to Heaven,' connotes
> that when all resources and the ability to at-
> tain justice on earth are exhausted, an appeal
> to earth's ultimate judge is the final recourse.
> This concept would become a foundational phi-
> losophy in American society, used even in the
> Declaration of Independence.[5]

The flag became famous throughout the colonies as General Washington's navy began winning significant battles against Great Britain's mighty navy. It is believed that the colonists' appeal to heaven invoked divine providence, which more than compensated for their lack of great military, weaponry, and wealth that Britain had.

The evergreen tree displayed on the flag refers to the time when a great Iroquois leader united five warring native tribes. The leader made them *bury their hatchets* underneath a great evergreen tree, "The Tree of Great Peace," a symbol of peace. It is believed that "due to the Iroquois' influence, the 'eternal' and 'covenantal' evergreen was placed on the Appeal to Heaven flag as a symbol of our nation's covenant with God, and possibly of our Founders' commitment to each other."[6]

Evergreen trees have always symbolized *eternity* since the time of Abraham. In Genesis 21:33, Abraham called upon *Olam El, the Everlasting God*, to witness a covenant he had made with King Abimelech. To "seal the deal," he planted a tamarisk tree, an *evergreen*. By *calling* on the *Everlasting God* and *planting* an *evergreen* tree, Abraham *wore both gloves*, consistent with Dutch Sheets' dream. As Dutch said in his book *An Appeal to Heaven*, "Pardon my Texas slang, but—*you can't make this stuff up!*"[7]

I thought about why the Lord had given me another wonderful "divine appointment" by introducing me to the "An Appeal to Heaven" flag, then I resolved that the book that He had given me was not to be centered solely around the destiny of a *tree*, but also about *our* individual destinies and that of our *nation*. I then trusted that, just as evergreen trees were used in the days of Abraham to seal covenants, and an evergreen tree was rendered on a flag 250 years ago to inspire and encourage our founding fathers in their fight for freedom, God just might want to use an *evergreen tree* once again to point the way to the *destiny* that He desires for our great nation!

As with the other "divine appointments" contained in this book, I believe that the Lord gave me the boxing gloves newspaper article so that I would discover the "An Appeal to Heaven" flag and how that wonderful story behind it *connects* with *Destiny of a Tree*.

Concerning the connections, the first and most obvious link is the prominent role the *evergreen tree* plays in both the book and the flag. Secondly, I believe it is very significant that *dreams* conveyed the messages that sent both Dutch Sheets and me on wonderful journeys that resulted in books being published *for God's glory*! And lastly, I further believe that the *most important* connection is my agreement with a conviction held by author Dutch Sheets, which he shared in his book: God has not written America off! Instead, He plans to use this nation to jumpstart the world into the last great *end-time revival* that will usher in His Son's triumphant *return* to earth!

CHAPTER FIVE

Divine Appointment Five

The Jack Pine Tree's Destiny

As mentioned in this book's introduction, the principal character of the poem that the Lord gave me, the jack pine tree, does, in fact, have a *destiny in real life*: it has distinguishing characteristics that point to Jesus Christ in *nine different ways!*

A jack pine tree is not your typical "Christmas Tree," which you would want to proudly display in your living room or family room. It is a small-to-medium-sized pine tree that is somewhat scraggly looking. It quickly loses the pyramid shape characteristic of a young pine and then assumes an open, slightly irregular crown. Besides, they do not usually grow perfectly straight, resulting in an irregular shape.

More than 99 percent of the jack pine trees growing in the US are located in the Great Lake states. They prefer rocky and sandy soils, unsuitable for most plants to bloom. Uniquely adapted to exist and reproduce on the hottest and driest sites in Michigan, they thrive on dune sand and the sandy glacial plains.

Characteristics one and two:

Feature number one and two are as follows: (1) its less-than-handsome appearance and (2) preference for less-than-fertile soil. I believe that these two characteristics of the jack pine tree point to Jesus as He is described in Isaiah 53:2 (TLB), "In God's eyes he was like a tender green shoot, sprouting from a root in *dry and sterile ground*. But in our eyes, there was *no attractiveness at all*, nothing to make us want him."

Characteristic three:

While the cones of other pine trees point downward, toward the ground, the cones of the jack pine point upward, as if watching for Jesus' return to earth to collect His bride, as Jesus Himself states in Matthew 25:13 (NKJV): "*Watch* therefore, for you know *neither the day nor the hour* in which the Son of Man is *coming*."

Characteristic four:

Jack pine trees provide a home and food source for certain animals and birds and wood for paper, fuel, decking, and utility poles. They are also a source of pinosylvinean, an antibiotic, and thus used in medicine to treat skin diseases, bronchitis, and wounds. I believe that this medical use of the jack pine tree points to Jesus. "How?" you might ask. Matthew 4:23 (NKJV) states: "Now Jesus went about all Galilee, teaching in their synagogues, preaching the gospel of the kingdom, and *healing all kinds of sickness and all kinds of disease* among the people."

Characteristics five and six:

While the other pine trees start dropping their cones once they are two years old, some of the jack pine's cones stay on the tree for many years. These *serotinous* cones are coated with a hard resin keeping the seeds inside until heat, usually from a forest fire, melts the covering. When the fire *kills the trees* and burns itself out, the cones open, and their *winged seeds* flutter to the ground, where the ashes from the burned trees have made a good bed for new seedlings. The seeds can then take root and *heal the land!*

This characteristic of this wonderful "guardian of the forest," i.e., sacrificing its life to save and heal the forest, points to Jesus who gave His life to save and heal others, as stated in 1 Peter 2:24 (NKJV), "Who Himself bore our sins in His own body *on the tree*, that we, having died to sins, might live for righteousness—by whose stripes *you were healed.*"

Also, the fact that the jack pine's cones have winged seeds indicates yet another description of Jesus according to Malachi 4:2 (NKJV): "The Sun of Righteousness shall arise with *healing in His wings.*"

Characteristic seven:

Another remarkable thing about this tree that points to Jesus is found in its *botanical* name: *Pinus banksiana lamb.* "Lamb" here refers to Aylmer Lambert, the British botanist who first described the jack pine in his *Description of the Genus Pinus.* According to the rules of the botanical nomenclature, the botanical name of a plant is supplemented with the abbreviated name of the author who first published the name. And fittingly, in the case of the jack pine tree, the abbreviated name of the author, "Lamb," points to Jesus, who is depicted in John 1:29 (NKJV) as "The *Lamb* of God who takes away the sin of the world."

Characteristic eight:

Another way through which this extraordinary tree points to Jesus Christ can be found in its *common name*: jack pine. It is believed that the name "jack" was given to this tree due to its early usefulness in making wooden jacks and levers. And just as jacks and levers multiply our strength tremendously, thereby enabling us to move obstacles and lift extremely heavy weights, when we call upon Jesus, He will give us the strength we need to get through all the trials and tribulations that this world has to offer. Calling upon Jesus empowers the accomplishment of things that would not be possible without the grace of God!

> In 2 Corinthians 12:9 (NKJV), Jesus said, "My grace is sufficient for you, for My *strength* is made *perfect* in weakness."

> First John 4:4 states (NKJV), "You are of God, little children, and have *overcome* them, because He who is in you is *greater* than he who is in the world."

> And Isaiah 40:31 (NKJV) proclaims, "But those who wait on the LORD shall *renew* their *strength*; they shall *mount up* with wings like eagles, they shall *run* and *not be weary*, they shall *walk* and *not faint*."

Furthermore, a *hydraulic* jack is a jack that uses a liquid, such as water or oil, to magnify its strength, thus giving it the *power* to lift tons of weight. Water and oil are essentially symbols of the *Holy Spirit* that speak of His *power* to anoint for service. Moreover, when we are filled with the Holy Spirit, as Jesus and His believers were in the Bible, God and Jesus can work through us to spread the Gospel and perform miracles of healings and deliverances as in Bible times. The following Bible passages attest to this:

> "But you shall receive *power* when the *Holy Spirit* has come upon you; and you shall be witnesses to Me in Jerusalem, and all Judea and Samaria, and to the end of the earth" (Acts 1:8, NKJV).
>
> "How God anointed Jesus of Nazareth with the *Holy Spirit* and with *power*, who went about *doing good* and *healing* all who were oppressed by the devil, for God was with Him" (Acts 10:38, NKJV).

Characteristic nine:

The jack pine tree points to Jesus in yet another way through its unique relationship with a pretty little songbird, the Kirtland's Warbler, considered one of the rarest birds on earth. These "firebirds" migrate from the Bahamas, Turks, and Caicos Islands each spring to nest *only* in the *jack pine* forests of Northern Michigan, Michigan's Upper Peninsula, Wisconsin, and Ontario (Canada), and *nowhere else* on earth. "They are very picky about where they live. Kirtland's Warblers need jack pine trees, and jack pine trees need fire."[8]

The warblers' nests are found only below the branches of five-to-twenty-year-old jack pine forests in mixed vegetations of grasses and shrubs. Ninety percent of the birds are found in Northern Michigan, with the largest concentration in Hartwick Pines State Park in Grayling, Michigan, where the Michigan Audubon Society conducts free daily tours from the end of May through the month of June for hundreds of bird watchers from over forty states and several other countries.

Just as this diminutive warbler, weighing no more than a pencil, *depends exclusively* upon the *jack pine* forest to meet its rigid habitat needs for nesting and thus the continued life of its species, *Jesus* is *the only way* to achieve an *everlasting life* with our Father God! John 14:6 (NKJV) states: "I am the *way*, the *truth*, and the *life. No one comes* to the Father *except through Me.*" While processing the significance of these marvelous revelations about how this amazing tree points to Christ, the Lord gave me yet another *appointment*!

The Prophet

CHAPTER SIX

Divine Appointment Six

The Harbinger Connection

The Harbinger is a New York Times Best-Seller novel that has sold over a million copies. It was written by Rabbi Jonathan Cahn, a Messianic Jewish Believer (a Jewish follower of Jesus) who leads Hope of the World ministries and the Jerusalem Center/Beth Israel worship center in Wayne, New Jersey.

In his book, Rabbi Cahn compares the 9/11 attacks that destroyed the Twin Towers of the World Trade Center with the account in Isaiah 9:8–12. According to the passage, God vowed to destroy ancient Israel because of two things: (1) ignoring His warnings and (2) not repenting for their sins. Though the book is a work of fiction, it managed to present a real-life connection between ancient Israel's destruction and the possible destruction of the United States.

Additionally, a journalist named Nouriel, one of the book's characters, meets a mysterious, unnamed "prophet" who, throughout the book, hands him nine ancient *seals*, all of which relate to the warning God gave Israel in Isaiah 9:8–12. At the end of the book, Nouriel is commissioned to write the prophetic message of the harbingers as a story in the form of a book—as "a watchman on the wall," whose duties are described in Ezekiel 33:6.

Rabbi Cahn maintains that just as Israel received a series of warnings before the ultimate judgment from God, *nine* events and facts concerning the 9/11 attacks against the US in 2001 were *harbingers* or warnings of possible impending judgment from God to America. The harbingers described in the book tie in *precisely* with the specific omens and signs given in the ancient biblical warnings!

As I approached the end of the amazing journey that the Lord took me on in the writing of *Destiny of a Tree*, He gave me yet another *divine appointment*: an assignment to read Rabbi Cahn's wonderful book, *The Harbinger*. As I read through the pages of the book and later learned how it came into being, I recognized several ways in which Rabbi Cahn's *book* has a connection with the one *God gave me!*

First of all, the principal character in the story that the Lord gave me was the jack pine tree, an *evergreen*. Correspondingly, the principal character of the book's seventh harbinger was the erez tree, also an *evergreen*. Isaiah 9:10 speaks of rebellious Israel: instead of repenting and turning to God, they elected and vowed to replace the feeble sycamores, which had been cut down by the invading armies, with the much bigger, stronger, and majestic *erez* cedars of Lebanon, which were *evergreens.*

Fascinatingly, the sycamore tree felled by the blast from the collapse of the North Tower was replaced by a *spruce tree*, an *evergreen* of the *Pinaceae* family—a sister tree of the cedar of Lebanon and the *jack pine tree!*

Another connection I could discern was how *Destiny of a Tree* and *The Harbinger* came into being. Rabbi Cahn compares the writing of his book with the pieces of a puzzle coming together. He stated that the fallen sycamore tree of 9/11 was the first piece of the puzzle [revelation] given to him. As he stood at ground zero viewing the tree, something inside of him hinted that there was something there, and he *must seek it out!* From that time on, *The Harbinger* took on a life of its own—every time he needed a piece to make his narrative, something would happen, or someone would say a word that provided the next piece of the puzzle.

Destiny of a Tree followed a similar vein. Just as Rabbi Cahn was told that there was something there that he *must seek out*, the Lord told me in my dream that what I saw was *beautiful to behold*, thus a story that *needs to be told!* In fact, we were *both* viewing a *tree* when we received our first revelations!

In the following days, months, and years, the simple but beautiful story that He gave me took on a "life of its own," as did Rabbi Jonathan Cahn's. On many occasions, I would remark to friends and family members that I had just found another "piece of the puzzle"!

Lastly, another connection between *Destiny of a Tree* and *The Harbinger* can be found in chapter 5, "The Jack Pine's Destiny." This chapter illustrates the *nine ways* that the jack pine tree, in *real life*, points to *Jesus Christ*. I believe that God is saying that His Son, *Jesus*, is *the answer* to *all* of the *nine harbingers* of Rabbi Cahn's book as brought forth through *Destiny of a Tree*!

I am convinced that just as the Nation of Israel came into being as God's chosen people, our wonderful nation, the United States of America, was also chosen to be birthed with Judeo-Christian roots. Ours was chosen to be the *city on the hill*, sending forth its beacon to welcome the poor and disadvantaged and to send *the Gospel* forth to the world.

In his "Message To America" Keynote Address at the Presidential Inaugural Breakfast on January 21st, 2013, Rabbi Cahn stated,

The city on the hill has grown darkened. Its lamp has grown dim. Its glory is fading, for God is not mocked. As it once was in Israel, the city on the hill now stands under the shadow of judgment.

The presence of the harbingers is not to *consign* a nation to judgment, but to *awaken* it to redemption; but in the message to return, the Voice of God is calling this nation in prayer, in humility, in repentance, and in hope. The word in Hebrew for safety and salvation is *Yeshewa*. Yeshewa is the name that we know in English as *Jesus*.

Outside of Him, there is no safety, but inside of Him, there is no fear. It was for Him, and in His Name, that this civilization, the city on a hill named America, came into existence, and it's *only* in Him and in His name that these problems can openly be answered. He remains the light in the darkness, the hope after all other hopes are gone; and to all who come, He will receive, and *He* calls, '*I will come.*'[9]

As I paused to contemplate why God used a *tree* from a dream in such a way to reveal His Son, Jesus, in such a time as this, as the answer to our world's problems, I was presented with another *divine appointment* via a CD that related how *extensively* God has *used* trees, parts of trees, and the products of trees throughout the Bible!

CHAPTER SEVEN

Trees in the Bible

Recently, I chatted with a man who has spent most, if not all, of his working years as a lumberjack in northern Michigan. When I remarked that I had heard that there are lots of jack pine trees in Northwest Michigan, he reacted in no uncertain terms that they are "good-for-nothing, worthless trees!"[10]

I believe that this man's negative opinion of the jack pine tree was a confirmation of characteristic one in chapter 6: the tree's less than handsome appearance points to Jesus as "having no attractiveness at all." I find it *very interesting* that the Father God would use such a "worthless" tree to point to His beloved Son in such wonderful ways as outlined in this book! Furthermore, this reminded me of John 1:46 (KJV), in which Nathanael asked Philip, "Can there any good thing come out of Nazareth?"

I also believe it is altogether fitting that the Father God would choose the lowly jack pine tree instead of a mighty oak or a majestic California redwood, in much the same way that He chose to have His beloved Son born in a humble stable instead of a majestic palace befitting the only begotten Son of the Creator of the universe!

Throughout the Bible, trees and their parts and products, such as branches, vines, fruits, and oils, were afforded prominent places physically, spiritually, figuratively, and symbolically. The word for *God* in Hebrew, "*El*," has a root linked to the word for "*tree*," as in the mighty oak. The Messiah in Hebrew prophecy is called *The Branch* because He's going to *branch* out to the world, as stated in The Living Bible Paraphrased version:

> The royal line of David will be cut off, chopped down like a tree; but from the stump will grow a Shoot—yes, a new Branch from the old root. And the Spirit of the Lord shall rest upon him, the Spirit of wisdom, understanding, counsel and might; the Spirit of knowledge and of the fear of the Lord.
>
> **Isaiah 11:1–2 (TLB)**

In John 15, Jesus teaches about the *Vine*, the *Gardener*, the *branches*, and the *fruit*:

> I am the true Vine, and my Father is the Gardener. He lops off every branch that doesn't produce. And he prunes those branches that bear fruit for even larger crops.
>
> **John 15:1–2 (TLB)**

Yes, I am the Vine; you are the branches. Who-
ever lives in me and I in him shall produce a
large crop of fruit. For apart from me you can't
do a thing. But if you stay in me and obey my
commands, you may ask any request you like,
and it will be granted.

John 15:5, 7 (TLB)

In his *The Divine Mysteries* CD/DVD album, Rabbi
Jonathan Cahn teaches about how God uses trees to sym-
bolize both the physical and the spiritual lives of Israel.[11]
He states that the *fig tree* represents the *physical* life of
Israel. In the Book of Hosea, the Lord declared that He
saw Israel's fathers as the first ripe figs of the tree. Jeremiah also speaks of the good figs and the bad figs, and Jesus
cites the parable of the fig tree that was given four years
to bear fruit.

While the fig tree is a symbol of the physical life of
Israel, the *olive tree* represents the *spiritual blessings* life
of Israel. Psalm 52:8 (KJV) states: "But I *am* like a green
olive tree in the house of God: I trust in the mercy of God
for ever and ever."

While the Jewish people are the *natural* branches of
the "*olive tree*," Apostle Paul, as a special messenger to

the *Gentiles* in Romans 11:13–24, tells them how they, as believers in God, have been *grafted in*: "So now you, too, receive the blessing God has promised Abraham and his children, sharing in God's rich nourishment of his own special olive tree" (Romans 11:17, TLB).

According to the sacred tradition of the Eastern Orthodox Church, the True Cross upon which Jesus was crucified was made from three different types of wood: cedar, pine, and cypress—all *evergreen* sister trees of the *jack pine*!

That *cedar* used in the crucifixion is supported in Scripture: The Old Testament is full of prophecies and references pointing to the coming Messiah. One such reference can be found in Leviticus 14:1–7. This passage details the instructions God gave Moses for the cleansing of lepers who have been healed, a foreshadowing of Jesus' crucifixion and resurrection. Among the eight elements to be included in the ceremony was a piece of *cedar wood*. Other elements were blood, water, an earthen vessel, scarlet, and hyssop—each of these elements symbolizes a component of the coming crucifixion—while two birds (one dead and one living) were used to foreshadow the coming Messiah's death and resurrection.

In all, twenty-seven different species of trees are mentioned in the Bible. Moreover, of the seventy parables in the New Testament, thirteen deal with trees or the products of trees. It is notable that the majestic cedar of Lebanon's high quality, pleasant scent, and resistance to both wood-destroying insects and rot made it King Solomon's wood of choice for his palace and the Lord's Temple in Jerusalem.

So, once again, the Father God, in His ultimate wisdom, has chosen to use yet another *tree* to achieve His divine purposes on earth as He did so many times in the Bible. In such a time as this, He chose to unveil the unique characteristics that He endowed the lowly jack pine tree with during its creation to reveal His beloved Son as the *only answer* to a lost and dying world in a *whole new way*! I believe that He has given us this simple tree, a product of nature we can see and touch, to beautifully illustrate the characteristics of His Son, whom He sent to earth as the ultimate sacrifice for our redemption!

Conclusion

The Greatest Revival

I believe that the *main thrust* and *purpose* of this book is to point out how *desperately* our nation and the entire world are in need of a *revival*! I'm not talking about just "another" revival like we have had in the past; although they have been wonderful, I refer to *the revival*! The huge last *earth-shaking end-time revival* that will result in Jesus fulfilling His role as Husband of the church and returning to earth to claim His bride as a glorious church, with neither spot nor wrinkle, but being holy and without blemish, as described in Ephesians 5:27.

In their book, *The World's Greatest Revivals*, authors Fred and Sharon Wright define "revival" based on this definition they received from the Lord:

> Revival is the divine reaction that spills over into time as hungry, desperate men rediscover key truths about God, His person, and His purposes that permeate and change the face of His Church and, through His Church, the world.[12]

In their book, the Wrights share the fascinating history of the four major "tsunami wave" revivals that have occurred in the last 600 years since the Dark Ages. Additionally, the book highlights a very interesting fact: the years *between* consecutive tsunami revival occurrences *shorten* as time progresses! It is also noted in the book that "many voices are being raised up about the Bride and the Bridegroom, and the groundswell of truth coming our way shows that the tsunami factor just might be in its very early stages of preparation for the *next outpouring*."[13]

The Wrights further stated that,

> The challenge now is to saturate ourselves in the love of the Father so that we will be ready for the next main event in the history of the Church. We need to be ready, fully filled with the Father's love for Jesus, passionately in love with our Bridegroom, Jesus, and eager for the Marriage Feast of the Lamb. The Bride and the Bridegroom represent the consummation of this age.[14]

I subscribe to Dr. Dutch Sheets' following statement: "When God came in and set up His plan for America, it wasn't just about *us*, it was for *everyone!* God needs this nation for what he is going to do for the Harvest of the Ages."[15]

I also agree with Rabbi Jonathan Cahn that God has raised America to be a light for all nations, and He is not finished with America. In a prayer he gave during an interview on the *Jim Bakker Show*, Rabbi Cahn mentioned that 9/11 was a *warning* to our nation and a *window* for *revival*. It was an opportunity for us to move, rise up, shine, and boldly *spread the Gospel* in an uncompromised manner. It was a window for us to repent of our sins and shortcomings so that we could rise to the hour unhindered in any way.

Moreover, I believe Abraham Lincoln's speech that he gave just before the Battle of Gettysburg is just as relevant today as it was then. Lincoln stated in his address that he did not doubt that our country would come through the Civil War safely and undivided. Nonetheless, his conviction was not rooted in the patriotism of the people, the bravery and devotion of the Union soldiers, or even the loyalty and skill of his generals. Lincoln proclaimed that the God of our fathers, Who raised our country up, would not let it perish now; God would bring us through safely, even though he [Lincoln] did not expect to see this come to fruition in his lifetime.

In conclusion, it all boils down to what God told Solomon after he had finished dedicating the Lord's Temple he had built for Him:

> If My people who are called by My name will humble themselves, and pray and seek My face, and turn from their wicked ways, then I will hear from heaven, and will forgive their sin and heal their land.

> **2 Chronicles 7:14 (NKJV)**

Just as it was the *destiny* of a *certain tree* to be stained by the blood of the *Son of God* over two thousand years ago, when He gave His life to save a broken world, it is fitting that it's the *destiny* of yet another *tree* to point the way to that *very Son* as the *only hope* for this lost nation and world to find it's way to the *Last Great Revival*. This is the revival that will prepare the bride of Christ to be free of every spot and wrinkle (thus holy and righteous before the Lord) in ushering in His return to earth and *claiming His bride*! *May He come quickly*!

EPILOGUE

What's *Your* Destiny?

Dear reader, as I reflect on this wonderful journey that the Lord took me on over the last nine years, I am amazed that a simple poem about a tree He gave me in a dream could *branch out* (pun intended) in so many directions, a consequence of which is this book!

The poem mentioned above posed a question: how could the destiny of a tree apply to both you and me? As noted in the previous chapter, I believe that the crux of the destiny story is to point the way to the *Last Great Revival* that will bring about the *Consummation of this Age*. Also, besides helping our great nation fulfill *its* destiny in God's grand plan, this book was also birthed to help *you*, dear reader, find *your* God-given *destiny!*

I am subscribed to *Mel's Video of the Day*, a daily email video service. The video I received on October 2nd, 2014, was titled "The Meaning of Life, Explained By A 6-Year-Old," the message of which I believe deserves to be repeated in this book:

How sad would it be to get to the end of your

life and realize that you never truly *lived*!
You're not going to do over life, so live your
dreams. You don't have to be great to get started, but you have to get started to be great![16]

Studies show that the biggest regret elderly people
have on their deathbed is not what they did; it's what they
didn't do—the risks they never took. Sadly, many people
go through life without *finding out* what their *God-Given*
destiny *is*, let alone fully enjoying life by walking in that
destiny!

Contrariwise, how wonderful it is for those who wake
up each morning anxious to get to work to enjoy *pursuing
their passion*! *You can be one of these people!*

As previously mentioned in this book's introduction,
our *loving Father God* does not randomly select a purpose
for putting you on planet earth and then, in effect, say,
"You can take it from here!" It is His *great desire* to guide
you, direct you, nurture you, and assist you in *untold ways*
to help you arrive at the destination He intended for you.
Hence, you can walk in the fullness of enjoying *heaven on
earth* while, at the same time, accomplishing *His works*
on earth through the gifts that He has bestowed upon *only
you*!

In writing his Psalms, Israel's great King David had

this to say about how God has blessed him and guided his life:

> The Lord will work out his plans for my life—for your loving kindness, Lord, continues forever.

Psalm 138:8 (TLB)

> You saw me before I was born and scheduled each day of my life before I began to breathe. Every day was recorded in your book! How precious it is, Lord, to realize that you are thinking about me constantly!

Psalm 139:16–17 (TLB)

David had the *destiny* to become the *greatest king of Israel*! And he was only able to fulfill this destiny because of his *relationship* with his Father God. You see, it's all about the *relationship*! Like many characters in the Bible, David was a *flawed* individual who made some grievous mistakes, but he was so quick to repent and ask for forgiveness whenever he erred that God called him *a man after His own heart*!

Acts 10:35 states that God is *no respecter of persons.* This means that inasmuch as He helped David, a little shepherd boy from a sleepy little village called Bethlehem, achieve his God-given destiny, God *desires* to help you achieve *yours.*

According to John 17:23, God the Father loves you and everyone else *just as much* as He loves His only be-gotten Son Jesus. In praying for His disciples and all future believers, Jesus tells His Father that He wants *all of them* to spend eternity with Him in heaven. In John 17:26 (TLB), He states: "And I have revealed you to them, and will keep on revealing you so that the mighty love you have for me may be *in them*, and *I* in *them.*"

If you haven't accepted Jesus as your Savior, I encourage you to do so today by admitting that you are a sinner and genuinely sorry and ashamed of your sins. You must then accept Jesus as the Christ, the Son of the Living God, who died on the cross to pay the price for your sins, therefore believing that Jesus has the power and love to save you and trusting Him to make you right with God. Confess that "*Jesus is Lord*" and invite Him into your life to be your Lord and Savior. Give Him the permission to change your life for the better, and then thank Him for all *He's done* and all *He's going to do*!

To decide where you will spend *eternity* is the *most important decision* you will *ever make* in this life. As a

WHAT IS *YOUR* DESTINY?

Christian, the Almighty God, the Master of the universe, is your *heavenly Father*, and you are a *joint heir* with *your spiritual Brother, Jesus*, of the *kingdom of God*, of *salvation*, of *righteousness*, and of *eternal life*!

In His parable about *The Lost Sheep*, Jesus shows that His Father sent Him to earth to save that which was lost, and it is not the will of the Father that one of these should perish (see Matthew 18:11–14).

Dear reader, I know that this may seem too simple, too good to be true, and too "pie in the sky," but I encourage you to do what King David asks of you in Psalm 34:8 (KJV): "O taste and see that the LORD is good: blessed is the man that trusteth in him."

Do not misunderstand; however, the Lord does not "promise you a rose garden" while you are here on earth. We are living in a sinful and fallen world, and Christians are not exempt from trials and tribulations. Notwithstanding, in Revelation 21:6–7, God the Father states:

> I am the Alpha and the Omega, the Beginning and the End. I will give of the fountain of the water of life freely to him who thirsts. He *who overcomes* shall inherit all things, and I will be his God and he shall be My son.

Revelation 21:6–7 (NKJV)

71

As a Christian, we can *call upon* and *rely upon* Jesus and the Holy Spirit to help us get through the trials and tribulations that may come our way. In 2 Corinthians 12:9 (NKJV), Jesus says, "My grace is sufficient for you, for My strength is made perfect in weakness."

Also, in Philippians 4:19 (NKJV), the Apostle Paul states, "And my God shall supply all your need according to His riches in glory by Christ Jesus."

So, dear reader, please take King David at his word. *Taste and see* how *your* life will change *for the better* as you trust in Jesus and learn to follow His ways as presented in the Bible. In addition to being your Savior, He can be your *Healer*, your *Deliverer*, your *Advocate*, your *Best Friend* if you will only *spend time with Him* and get to *know Him intimately*!

Your whole outlook on life will change as you continue your Christian walk. You will have greater compassion for people with whom you come in contact—even strangers. You will have a greater appreciation for God's creations: butterflies, hummingbirds, a fragrant rose. You will marvel at things you once took for granted: a beautiful sunrise or sunset, the scent of newly fallen rain on a spring morning, a campfire on a midsummer's night, the blazing color of a forest in late October, the way freshly fallen snow glitters under the full moon!

As your fellowship with the Lord becomes even more *intimate*, you will begin to notice *miracles* happening in your life: small miracles, medium-sized miracles, large miracles, but *miracles indeed*! You will look back and say, "No way! There's no way that could have happened!" *But it did!* Then you will realize, yes, God loves you so much that He will work an honest-to-goodness *miracle* just *for you*!

In Matthew 7:11, Jesus states that if hard-hearted, sinful men know how to give good gifts to their children, how much more shall your Father, who is in heaven, give good things to them that ask Him? My wife and I have noticed that many of the wonderful miracles that we have been blessed with have resulted from fervent prayer, but others have been *totally unexpected*—beautiful *gifts* from our Father's *inconceivable love* for us!

Gifts like coming home from getting a haircut and finding a $600 Nikon camera sitting on our dining room table! Gifts like a $900 adult three-wheeler bike that gave my legally blind wife a kind of freedom that she never thought possible! Gifts like the Lord providing nine vehicles over the last thirty years so that we wouldn't have to pay any car loan payments!

When God created you, He endowed you with certain *gifts* designed to help you achieve the *purpose* for which you were destined. Some reactions to this might be along the lines of, "Yeah, I used to think I had a special destiny, but nothing's been happening!" You may think your promise is dead and your destiny is finished.

I agree with the following statement made by Dr. Doug Sheets: "It's never too late for God to bring back His promises for you. Expect for God to move in new ways, wonderful ways in your life."[17] God's plan for your life does not change. It's *always available*! He doesn't take His gifts back. It's up to you to use them. If you use them for His glory, He will bless you *and* your efforts.

God acts on behalf of us who *wait upon Him* to help us fulfill our destiny—to allow Him to *live in us*, to keep us in step with His *timing* for us. *Timing is everything!* In Jeremiah 29:12–13 (TLB), God says, "In those days when you pray, I will listen. You will find me when you seek me, if you look for me in earnest."

And the Psalmist had the following to add:

> Lord, if you keep in mind our sins, then who
> can ever get an answer to his prayers? But you

forgive! What an awesome thing this is! That is why *I wait expectantly*, trusting God to help, for he has promised.

Psalm 130:3–5 (TLB)

Isabel Allum runs an international prophetic ministry based out of her Forest City Destiny Church in London, Ontario. She has this to say about receiving your kingdom destiny:

> There is nothing in life that compares to knowing what you were born to be, why you exist, and attaining it. When you experience this, everything changes, rest comes to your soul and success to your life. We want you to realize that it is possible for ordinary people to live the extraordinary lives that they were created for. We are fulfilling the destiny God created us for and we know, without a doubt, that He is longing for all of His children to live their kingdom life and receive their kingdom destiny."[18]

In summary, I believe that the poem "Trees," the song "The Three Bells," and the novel, *The Harbinger* were all *inspired, ordained,* and *anointed* by God to achieve the fame and fortune that have been afforded to them. I also believe that the *divine appointments* that were given to Carol and me in bringing the book, the song, and the poem to our attention were how God encouraged us and let us know that He is *behind this project*!

It is indeed a humbling experience to know that the Master of the universe *can and will* work hand-in-hand with you to give you a vision for a project such as this book and then supernaturally help you *bring it to fruition.*

Carol and I are in excited anticipation to see what the Lord does with this book, and we pray that you, the reader, will have found something in the foregoing pages that will open a door (or doors) to help you find the *destiny* that God has *planned for you* from the *beginning of time*!

Always remember, *God loves you*, and *so do we*! We have *tasted* and *seen*, and *God is good*!

ENDNOTES

1   Dr. Charles F. Stanley, *In Touch Ministries*, daily devotional, April 17, 2013.
2   "Trees" (poem). Retrieved from *Wikipedia*, the free encyclopedia.
3   Ibid.
4   *Okzonia* website.
5   Dutch Sheets, *An Appeal To Heaven*, (Dallas, TX: Dutch Sheets Ministries, 2015), 44.
6   Ibid, 49.
7   Ibid, 50.
8   Amy S. Hansen, *Fire Bird: The Kirtland's Warbler Story*, (Traverse City, MI: Arbutus Press, 2017), 30.
9   Rabbi Jonathan Cahn's "Message To America" Keynote Address at the Presidential Inaugural Prayer Breakfast on January 21, 2013. DVD Disc # 7 of Rabbi Cahn's *The Divine Mysteries* 11 CD/DVD album.
10 My personal interview with lumberjack Dean Pendock of Central Lake, Michigan, took place on June 28, 2017.
11 Rabbi Jonathan Cahn's *The Mystery Of The Ilanot*, CD #2 of his *The Divine Mysteries* 11 CD/DVD Album.
12 Fred and Sharon Wright, *The World's Greatest Revivals*, (Shippensburg, PA: Destiny Image, 2007), 43–44.
13 Ibid, 269.
14 Ibid, 269.
15 Dr. Dutch Sheets preaching at Pastor Chuck Pierce's church in Corinth, Texas. Video viewed on March 5, 2014.

16   *Mel's Video Of The Day*: www.coolestone.com, viewed on October 2, 2014.

17   Dr. Dutch Sheets, "Prophecy for 2014" sermon on CD, viewed on April 10, 2014.

18   Ivan and Isabel Allum, *Your Destiny, Unlocking The Impossible Promises Of God*, (Self Published by Ivan and Isabel Allum, Canada, 2007), 1–2.

CPSIA information can be obtained
at www.ICGtesting.com
Printed in the USA
JSHW030429070722
27658JS00001B/5

9 781685 565657